AF413400

The Wind and the Footprints

The Wind and the Footprints

A Story of Spiritual Transformation

By
JOHN MORROW

RESOURCE *Publications* · Eugene, Oregon

THE WIND AND THE FOOTPRINTS
A Story of Spiritual Transformation

Resource Publications
An Imprint of Wipf and Stock Publishers
199 W. 8th Ave., Suite 3
Eugene, OR 97401

www.wipfandstock.com

PAPERBACK ISBN: 979-8-3852-0392-5
HARDCOVER ISBN: 979-8-3852-0393-2
EBOOK ISBN: 979-8-3852-0394-9

VERSION NUMBER 122123

Contents

Acknowledgments

It has been quite a process to see this project come to fruition, and I am indebted to all of those who have come alongside me in my journey of faith to help me become who I am today. In many ways, this project is a reflection of my own journey, which could not be possible without other people within my community.

First, I wish to thank God for calling me and setting me apart to be on this journey of transformation as I attempt to abide in Christ and display the fruit of the Spirit. I thank God for inspiring me and for calling me to a life of contemplative reflection.

Secondly, I thank God for my wife, Angela, who is always there for me as a source of encouragement, and for my children, who teach me the values of life and priorities.

My journey of discipleship is attributed to far too many people for me to count. I am indebted to my father for originally teaching me how to slow down, be still in God's presence, and wait on the Lord. I must give thanks to Portland Seminary for the opportunity to study spiritual formation. Many of my reflective thoughts and questions have transpired from my time at Portland Seminary. My personal reflections from engaging in the formational experiences cultivated from Portland Seminary courses have played a significant role in generating contemplative thoughts for this work.

All the teachers at Portland Seminary who have invested significant time in me as a student are to be thanked. The Transformational Courses taught by Dr. MaryKate Morse were inspirational to me on this journey. I have learned to engage my own transformational journey and to struggle with discovering who I am uniquely shaped and formed to be.

Also, I must thank Dr. Rich Handley, my internship coach, for encouraging me to write, to cast vision for myself, and to reach my potential.

Finally, there are countless others. Too many to count, but there are those who have helped pave the way for it to be possible for me to arrive at where I am today, and I hope this project is evidence of the fruit of the investment of many others in my life who have shown me the way of Christ.

Introduction

Dear friend and fellow partner on this journey, as you prepare to read the following story, there might be a variety of reasons why you chose to pick up the book you are holding in your hand. Whether you realize it or not, if you have life and breath, then you are on a journey. I want to invite you into the story of the main character of the Wind and the Footprints.

Join Mathetes as he navigates through the challenges and possibilities awaiting him. I want you to be challenged to peel back the layers and find that the lessons within this story are more than what is depicted in the physical world around us, but rather, they illustrate deeper meanings found within the work of the soul. You will get the opportunity to eavesdrop on a raw dialogue between Mathetes and what is understood to be the Church. I want to invite you to engage this dialogue with an open mind and faithfully reflect on the critique and pushback as it relates to an understanding of a Church constantly redefining itself, if necessary, to better understand what it means to have personal salvation and to truly follow with faithful obedience.

You are also invited into the juxtaposition between walking this journey in community and doing the personal work of the soul that we, and only we, are responsible for individually. There are times when we need community and there are times when we take personal responsibility for the discipline required for formation and growth.

Introduction

I also invite you to consider that life is not only about the spiritual soul, but rather as we remember that there is a creation and there is a Creator, please consider the lessons this has to offer us. As you look around and ponder the beauty, lessons, and danger of creation, let them be our teacher and our source of wisdom.

Finally, life is not always merely about reaching the destination and it's not always a "what," but rather life is about "who." Reflect on these things, and I pray you might find guidance and insight into your own journey of following.

I am mindful that each of us will be on different stages of our journey and the timeline for every one of us will vary. However, I believe that the one who holds an outstretched hand to you and beckons you to follow will meet you where you are. If you can view life as a marathon and not as a sprint, then take moments to ponder the journey and not the destination.

May God bless you on this journey, and I pray that you might discover the true rewards of what it means to be in passionate pursuit of the trail left behind by our Master, and I pray you might discern the implications of the written words left for us. Finally, I pray you might find the discernible presence of the wind as you tune into these things and as you journey through life's greatest lessons both outwardly and inwardly. There is an interior being of the soul placed by our own Creator, and may you discover it as the true source, deep within your soul, providing meaning and purpose.

Blessings,
John Morrow

I. Beyond Comfort

When I lifted my eyes beyond the boundaries of the marketplace, I saw the mysterious one walking toward me. I fixed my gaze on him as he navigated through the noisy crowds of people as if he was not bound by time. While others hurried off to frantically tend to their business, he would pause to savor the aroma from the fresh cakes of bread roasting over a fire. As the smell arose to meet his nostrils, he closed his eyes and basked in the moment. Continuing past the baker, he paused to appreciate the handiwork of the carpenter.

The villagers know of this mysterious one. Indeed, his reputation has preceded his presence. A great multitude spoke about this great teacher and healer. He moves from village to village. I wonder how many of the rumors about him are true. How is one to know? It seems to me that the only way to truly know is to invest in the time needed to discern truth from error. Who are we to believe such things about others when there is no substantial evidence or credibility? What must we do to know and seek out the truth? We must take time to learn for ourselves. We can learn from others and we can personally invest in the process of learning, not to have knowledge for our minds, but also to have practical wisdom for the heart. I want to explore the depths of the truth surrounding this individual and to build upon that which I have already seen and heard.

My friend Ekklesia knows the mysterious one personally. She and I spent countless hours conversing about him. I would listen while she would share with me all about his great and marvelous deeds. Ekklesia embodies his presence in many ways. She models and reflects his image. Truly, one of the ways to make someone known is through imitation. I have often heard that we are shaped and formed to be like the individuals within the communities in which we dwell. Driven by this manifestation of his presence, deep within me there is a stirring. There is a hunger and thirst for more.

He was unlike any other teacher. Eyewitness accounts detailed how he would take children in his arms and bless them. The people who spent time soaking in his teaching would depart in awe and amazement by his words. Others broke bread with him. His acceptance of people made many feel welcomed and invited to his table. I pondered the meaning of his presence. He was like a breeze of life, flowing, flourishing, and transforming anything and everything he touched. There were stories and faint testimonies about him. Some have conveyed how an encounter with him calls for change and transformation. It is believed one cannot depart from his presence without being changed, or at least given the opportunity to journey toward an unknown destination of transformation. Now here he is. He is here. He is in our midst. He is moving through the marketplace.

What a privilege that he would pass by my humble fruit stand. I didn't have much to offer, but I offered what I had. I extended my hands toward him, clenching my fingers around the best cluster of grapes I could find. As I opened my hands to offer them to the mysterious one, he glanced at the grapes with a smile. His face displayed appreciation that I would offer such a gift, though I had so little. His response seemed to convey that while he was not in need of my gift, he knew it was from my heart. Indeed, he pierced my soul. He took the grapes and gave them to an individual in need who was seeking shelter from the sun beneath a canopy overhanging the marketplace. Turning once again toward me, he said, "Thank you," though not with his words. His gratitude came from the depth and sincerity of his eyes.

The gaze of this man pierced my weary soul. The expression on his face and the depths of his presence captivated me. He knew something, and I had yet to learn. He longed to share something without uttering a word; I sensed this deep within me. I believed with my whole heart that he knew me, and for all my life, I believed he knew my thoughts and all there is of me.

I pondered these questions: Where did he come from? Where was he going? Could he possess the secret to my life's deepest yearnings? I sensed an urgency to follow. I knew I needed to learn more about this mysterious one.

At first, I took a few steps away from my fruit stand just to have a better look. There was no commitment from me, but he kept moving. As I drifted further away from my business, I could see more clearly. As I fixed my eyes down the street to the place where he was, I spent a few moments in undivided attention. I noticed some peculiarities that made him different from others. When he spoke, people ceased their activities to listen. The sound of children laughing and playing in the marketplace was of little concern as he shared with others. He spoke; he listened; he was present. Children were noisy and distracting, yet he didn't respond. Both young and old were pleased by his presence.

The hustle and bustle of life in the marketplace began to fade to stillness. I fixated on his every word. I watched his every move. I said to myself, "Surely, I want to be like him."

Just then, a gentle breeze began to blow. It felt fresh. I found myself basking in the coolness of the wind. I lifted my head and closed my eyes to soak in the warmth of the sun as the cool breeze swept across my face. Then, I came back to my senses and realized the figure was on the move. He was leaving. Where was he going? I immediately ran after him. Catching his attention, I asked, "Where are you going?" He looked back as if to applaud my courageous step away from the familiar and into the unknown. With a smile, he replied, "Come! I will show you."

With this invitation, he kept moving, and for a brief moment I watched as the distance increased between us. My internal thoughts questioned my decision. Do I dare leave the familiar for the unknown? Where would we go? I stood there rather indecisively as I contemplated my next move. My mind began to process what it meant to be invited on this journey of following. He beckons me. I see the invitation from an unseen hand deep within me stretching out to invite me on this journey. There is obscurity to this idea of "calling," yet I find myself beginning to better understand. There is no place I can flee from this calling. If I were to dwell in the hustle of the noisy crowds, the still small voice inside and the invisible outstretched arm would still invite me to follow. This one thing I know. I am being summoned. If I were to ascend mountaintops, the calling would be there. If I were to flee across the outstretched land, there I would still be beckoned. I will choose to respond.

This village is a strange space to be in tune with such things. It is a space that has been set apart for humans to coexist in a symbiotic relationship. When one takes a moment to reflect on this space of community, we truly need one another. In the areas of my shortcomings, you have something to offer. Likewise, I have something within my possession that could be a benefit for you. This is the economic nature of our existence together. We have come together for the sake of survival within community. This is what we all share. We share the need for community, survival, and space to sustain our life through communal exchange and interaction. For this reason, our very marketplace exists. Why should this be disrupted? What could this figure offer that we don't already possess?

When this calling shows up in the most ordinary of spaces, we cannot help but be intrigued by a presence of something beyond our comprehension. In my mind I know what I need to do, but in my heart and soul, I see something with a set of eyes that just might be beyond all I could ever have imagined. I see something beyond the physical boundaries. As I lift my eyes toward the hills, I wonder what is beyond that geographical boundary and is it possible to go there? Indeed, I am thankful and content for the community of this space of exchange with fellow humans, but there is a deeper meaning to all of this, and of this, I want to know. Perhaps it will be found with this mysterious one. I need to follow.

I chose to follow from a distance. Navigating the streets, I observed him as he stopped to preach and teach. Following closely, I noticed something quite intriguing. While he would sit and teach the crowds, those who gathered received his preaching and teaching with gladness. However, then they packed up with his words and departed. I watched as they began to preach and tell others about him. I wondered to myself, "But do they know him?" Many of his followers were settling down in the village. I heard the clanking sound of hammers clashing against the metal stakes. I heard ropes tightening as followers pitched their tents, made their shelters, and set up their shops for the business of ministry. That is, the business of proclaiming the teaching and words of this mysterious one. After soaking in his words and teaching, they began to instruct others about the mysterious one, but it seemed to me that they ceased following him. The mysterious one kept moving.

For a while, I stood still and in silence. I wasn't sure what to do. As this master teacher, as he is known, kept moving, I found myself among his followers. They spoke passionately, and they proclaimed what they believed. I wanted more. Once again, I asked myself, "Why do I not wish to stay in the village and settle for the teaching like everybody else?" But deep inside, I knew the answer. It was not enough. I didn't know enough. I needed to know this person intimately, so I kept moving.

One by one, the crowd who followed the mysterious one began to dwindle. Instead, they began talking about him. Some imitated him. They wanted to be a living example of the "Son of Man," which is the title by which he would call himself while teaching. The followers were content and satisfied; it was as if they had arrived at all they wanted to know. They proclaimed to know God's will. But it wasn't enough for me. Great are the mysteries of this individual. How foolish to settle! I wanted more. I wanted to pursue him. I knew my next step would be the most courageous.

II. In Pursuit

When I came to the edge of our town, I stood for a few moments staring at the vast fields. The rolling hills in the distance stood between me and my journey. I saw where the hills met the sky. I watched as a silhouette of the Son of Man began to fade, leaving only a trail of footprints. I contemplated whether I would continue this journey. My heart sank as hope seemed to dwindle. I looked back at the crowds gathered on the streets of the village. For a moment, I was tempted to return to my business.

Suddenly, another gust of wind swept over me. It pushed against me more forcefully than the gentle breeze from before. I could hear it. It was rushing and thrusting my body forward. The force blew the stalks of grain. I watched as the sea of yellow swayed back and forth in the wind. On the edge of town, I stood still.

In that moment, I had to come face-to-face with vulnerability and uncertainty. How often in the past I held my heart out to others only to have it squashed, broken to pieces, and trampled on by those who do not have the capacity to hold sacred the best of what I have to offer. Do I dare offer my heart and risk disappointment?

While the lessons were not soon forgotten, I would not trust another person with my heart. The ache, the pain, the betrayal, the hypocrisy are all imprinted within my memory. What could this individual have that was different? As I took one more glance back at where I had been, I resolved within me that I needed to take a courageous step forward, but what would it take for me to respond?

Just then, a still small voice inside me cried out, "More!" I wanted more. I ran after him with my whole heart, but he was gone. I passed through the field of grain. Ascending the rolling hills, I arrived at the sea. He was gone! I looked across the sand until I saw footprints. With each step I could see his imprint in the sand. His footsteps forged a path near the edge of the water, as if to defy and taunt the boundaries of the great sea.

While my heart was racing, and while my focus was to relentlessly continue this path, I paused for a few moments to take in the beauty of the great sea surrounding me. I was torn with a tension deep inside of me. Although I felt the sense of urgency to keep going and to keep moving across the sandy beach, I couldn't help but acknowledge that there was a stillness that I needed to practice.

For a moment, I needed to rest and gaze out on that which I was too busy to notice. I took in the sounds of the mighty ocean crashing against the shore. I took in the sights of the mighty waves, breaker after breaker, forming off in the distance and then reaching the boundary where my feet stood. I took in the clouds rolling across the horizon and the sun ever so slightly peaking through the clouds to provide a moment of warmth.

And as I looked up, I took in the sights and sounds of the birds circling the water in search of food. There existed a juxtaposition in that moment. There was noise, yet it wasn't noise depicting the hustle of the marketplace. It was the noise of beauty; it was the noise of creation at work in this moment. It was the noise of wind, for though it is mighty, the birds themselves rely upon it to rise with wings into the spaces above, and they peer down on the world below them.

It was almost indescribable to express the peace and comfort I felt basking in the beauty of that space. As I looked out on the space of the mighty waters reaching the horizon, my mind began to drift. I began to see that which is unseen in this space. As the birds were diving into the water to pull out the catch of fish to feed them, I was reminded that beneath the surface of the waters, there is life. Beneath the surface, life is busy for the created living creatures dwelling below. How often do we pause to reflect on the fact that there is more going on beneath the surface than that which we can visibly see.

Beneath the surface, in the spaces of the unseen of our lives, there is life. When there appears to be nothing happening, we remember something is happening. I was pondering all the interactions I have had with others. I was beginning to wonder if I truly know others. Do I look at others in the way I gaze upon the surface of the deep waters? Is there more to others than I see? Regretfully, I have been too busy to notice. My prayer, "Oh Lord, grant that I may look out on the surface of others and understand the depths in such a way that I may know others better." How could I utter such a prayer without pondering such implications for myself?

There is depth to me. There is beauty and there is unsettled activity. "Oh Lord, as you gaze upon me, and as you know me, see the activity beneath the surface of my life. See the dwelling spaces longing to receive a touch of who you are and longing for rest and peace."

I wanted to stay in that moment. I was finding rest and peace within the presence of what was being offered and I was finding peace and comfort in this space. I allowed the water to wash over my feet and I felt the cold temperature. It awoke me to a heightened sense of awareness. I was aware; I was aware of the presence of that space.

I was beginning to understand this. As a part of my journey, I would need to continue the practice of being present to my surroundings and to be aware of the space where I was residing in any given moment. There is a lesson, and there is a space waiting to teach me. It is a lesson unlike any other space, for in other spaces, our lessons are delivered to us verbally. Or, our lessons are written in word form. Finally, at times, some of the greatest lessons in life are learned from mistakes and regrets. We look back on these spaces with regret.

However, in that moment, there was a teacher crying aloud for someone willing to listen and for someone willing to be present in that very moment. With a renewed sense of vision and awareness, I was ready to move on and continue my journey.

I got up from my place of rest and continued my pursuit of the footprints. As I watched the foamy waves crash against his footprints, not even the tide could remove the imprint of the Son of Man. I kept following, and I felt a renewed sense of confidence and courage.

A storm came, and the waves thrashed against the shore, but I still followed. The waves made his footprints appear faint. However, there was a familiarity with his steps. My own footsteps had fallen in sync with his. Gaining a renewed sense of confidence, my purpose was becoming clearer with every step, and by venturing down this path, I felt capable of taking on any challenge. The beauty of the sand and the ocean was enough to invite anyone to bask in the warm sun and cool breeze flowing from the sea. Following this man was good, and it brought me joy. I was ready to move into the water and cross the strength of the breakers if necessary. "Here I am," I thought to myself. "Lord, send me through the challenges of the raging sea," I cried in prayer. With full confidence, I felt called and equipped and zealous in my pursuit. From the safety of the shore, I believed I could do anything. Never in my whole life had I felt so confident and alive. Pride was creeping in on me as I was full of myself, my own confidence, and my own abilities.

I was blinded to the dangers of such pride and confidence. As with any journey, one begins with excitement and enthusiasm for the adventure that lies ahead. However, in time, we lose this sense of initial zeal and excitement, and on this journey the excitement will acquiesce to the focus of the destination. This is a dangerous space, for we fail to miss out on that which needs to be learned and acquired in each moment and with each passing step. My mind began to ponder moments when my focus on a destination caused me to miss out on opportunities to be present.

Furthermore, there is the element of pride seeping in as I taunt the mighty waves of the ocean. I pondered, "Who am I to be filled with such pride?" In all the beauty that the ocean has to offer, I respect its power and I respect its Creator, and this demands nothing less than for me to be humble.

I began to reflect on an encounter I had with a man who shared the story of his experience climbing a mountain. The man said, "Respect the mountain." This means with every move, and with every decision, there is a requirement of applying wisdom and discernment. In the same way, I don't command the wind and the mighty currents of nature in front of me. It is much more powerful than I could ever imagine. Rather, I respect it. Furthermore, I respect with awe and wonder the Creator behind the visible and known creation. Who am I to think any more highly of myself than I ought?

In this journey, as I began to feel proud and zealous to conquer mighty achievements, I knew such assertion of confidence could turn to reality in any given moment. The truth is this: I am not prepared to be the person I am meant to be. I am not equipped to do what I'm supposed to do. Truthfully, whether realizing it or not, I need a realistic perspective if I am to approach this journey further.

With this perspective, I continued. I thought it would be fitting to still my mind and my thoughts. As I followed the footprints along the great and mighty sea, I allowed there to be silence with my strides. I attempted to discipline the noisy thoughts racing in my mind to tell myself, "Be still in this moment." Admittedly, there was a sense of comfort in this. Although I was gaining a sense of a renewed and realistic perspective of myself, I acknowledged an incomplete work yet to be done inside of me as I anticipated another phase of my journey.

While I followed the footprints along the shore, this allowed me to continue to gaze upon the beauty of the waters, and the sun was beginning to set. My words failed to describe this beauty. The waters were sparkling as the sun was finding a place to rest beyond the horizon, and I saw the portrait of the beauty of creation. I knew it was time to keep moving, and I followed the footprints along the shoreline.

But then his footprints began to move away from the sea. The sand became dry. The wind was blowing the dry sand over the footprints until they disappeared. I followed the direction of the wind, for I knew it was blowing toward the Son of Man. I came to a timberline. The green trees created a place of hospitality and shade for such a hot day. But I knew the wind was beckoning me away from the timberline. For reasons beyond my comprehension, I was moving away from the comfort of a lush green environment and into a rugged and rough terrain in front of me, but I kept moving forward.

III. Through Barren Land

As I approached the rugged and rocky terrain of the barren wilderness, I questioned the path. Surely the mysterious figure and the man whom I'd been following didn't go this way. This barren wilderness was like a desert; it was hot, dry, and unpredictable. Dangers lurked behind every turn. In this environment there are warnings of snakes, scorpions, and sudden storms. This couldn't have been his purpose for me. I stepped over the threshold and continued my pursuit into dry land.

I sat under the shade of a palm tree to cool down and find relief from the heat of the sun. Doubts began to creep into my mind. "I want to go back," I uttered to myself. As I wrestled with the temptation to retreat from my journey, I lifted my eyes to the sky and fixed my gaze on a circling osprey above me. It swooped down and peered intently into the rocky crevices in search of food. I was amazed at how even the birds of the air find food in the wilderness. It reminded me that there is provision, and yet creation is searching for nourishment. I watched as lizards and rabbits hurried around the rugged and rocky terrain in search of food, and I was reminded about the great Provider. I started to ponder familiar writings about this figure. Who is like a shepherd to my soul on this journey? I knew my journey would help me find the answer. Continuing on my path, I found strength and motivation.

As I rose to my feet and looked toward the distant path in front of me, I saw the footprints. The Son of Man went through the rocky and rough terrain of the desert, but I didn't know why. I followed the footprints with my eyes until they disappeared over the horizon. I started walking. The ground was rough. There were huge boulders at every turn. Through uncertainty, I followed. I was cautious. With every step I knew I could easily stumble over a rock. I will never forget the intense heat of the sun beating down on my face. I often would stop to rest under the shade of palm trees; I rested in caves and wherever I could find refuge from the sun. However, after each rest, I kept moving.

The path I was on was becoming narrower. While the footprints continued through this wilderness, I could see the journey imprinted in the dirt. The journey was written in the dirt. The dust was so dry that it kicked up into the air with every imprint from my feet. I continued to pursue the footprints.

IV. Conversations with
the Faith Community

While stopping to rest, I saw a figure approaching from a distance. As the figure drew near to me, I recognized who it was. It was my friend Ekklesia. I watched as she cautiously navigated her way through the rugged terrain. She was leaning on her walking stick with every step to ensure solid footing for her steps. Her hair was long as it swayed in the breeze of the blowing wind. As I watched her hair flowing in the wind, I felt a sense of comfort. Seeing the movement of something invisible and yet filled with such force and strength reminded me of the great wisdom and strength often found through faith, even when faith in things unseen is required. When she looked at me, her gaze was filled with genuine care and compassion. She was fitted with a clean robe, though not perfect. I could still see rips, tears, and stains depicting perseverance through seasons of uncertainty. She carried a pouch of water both for her own thirst and to share with those in need. She also brought me bread for my journey. We spread out a space for us to commune in each other's presence; even in the space of this rugged terrain, it was suitable to meet, share, discuss,and ponder the deeper meanings in life.

I enjoyed the presence of Ekklesia. Prior to my journey, we spent time together. She shared stories and imparted to me wisdom about the One, also known as the Great Shepherd, Creator, and Provider, and she knew the mysterious figure whom I was following, also known as the Son of Man. It was always refreshing to visit together in her presence. We sat together on two rocks under the shade of the palm tree. We enjoyed refreshing drink and satisfying bread. Interesting it is that we did not need to be in a designated building to participate together in this fellowship. It wasn't long before we began to speak about my journey. We discussed at length my journey and my relationship with the koinonia—that is, the designated community for all who have decided to be taught by the Son of Man. We wrestled with difficult questions. We explored the depths of what it means to live a life in pursuit of the footprints and to follow the wind through both gentle breezes and at times with a mighty rushing force.

When the timing was right, she brought to the surface the throbbing question. She asked, "Mathetes, why are you here? The Son of Man has left the teaching we need. We have instructions. Come back with me and let us enjoy the koinonia as we gather together with one another. Let us enjoy the teachings of his very words. Let us remember all that was taught. Was it not during your time with the koinonia that you came to believe in the Son of Man? Come back with me. We will serve and please the One by all our good deeds, for this is God's will."

Her last five words were very unsettling to me. I didn't harbor bitterness toward my friend, but I was angry and hurt by her audacity. How could one so confidently claim to know the will of God? Who knows it, really? Is it known by hearing? Is it known by a journey of personal experience? Or, is it both?

If I returned with Ekklesia, we could once again bask in the comfortable and familiar surroundings while listening to the words taught by the Son of Man. However, I knew in my heart that the koinonia alone could not meet my deepest needs. I must follow, and I must be in a passionate pursuit.

Finally, I said, "Ekklesia, I love the koinonia. But I feel that I have neither seen nor heard the fullness of what it means to follow the Son of Man. I want more. I want to know the One who loves me. I want to know the One who created me. I want to know the One who says, 'Follow me,' and I want to know genuine and authentic love. I long for servanthood flowing from a heart of pure authenticity. I want to know honesty. I want to know true hospitality without the pride of performance and good deeds. Can these traits be found? Can I attain these attributes? For this reason, I am on this journey. By following the wind and pursuing the footprints, I will cling to the One, for that is God's will for me." I could see Ekklesia pondering these thoughts as she gazed into the vast scenery of the surrounding wilderness. Then, there was silence.

I broke the silence with these words: "Ekklesia, whom do you serve? Progress? Success? Do you strive to earn the favor and approval of people? When placed upon a scale, should individual good deeds outweigh personal transformation? Who will sit in the judgment seat to observe the tipping point? Perhaps we don't see the deficit of our own formation because we are too busy 'doing.' My friend, we have much to think about and consider. Is it the plan of the One to love progress and use people to pursue success? Or, is it for people to love and pursue the Son of Man, consequently, being conformed into his likeness?"

I continued to speak: "We must pursue and follow the essence rather than settle for the perceived presence. We must pursue the wind and become accustomed to its movement. Therefore, we should not pitch a tent over any footprint, because the Son of Man moves forward and the wind keeps blowing. Who knows the mind and movement of the One? Does the footprint of the Son of Man make us thirsty to follow? Or have we pitched a tent around the footprint to worship it? Shall we hold fast to where the Son of Man has been, as I observed in the village? Or do we grasp where the Son of Man is going even while the destination is not always clear?

On this journey, I fear ceasing to follow will cause me to lose sight of the Son of Man, and I will be tempted to produce my own idol. I do not wish to build up my own image of the One. We are prone to worship that which we can see, feel, touch, and measure. Are our hands clean of this practice in the koinonia? How do we continue in our pursuit of the invisible? Is it through a cloud by day beckoning us, and a fire by night in front of us? Do these lead us to a promised land? These elements are on the move. When they move, we as God's people should be challenged to also move.

Historically, in the wilderness, our ancestors kept moving, and should we not do the same?"

I continued, "Do you truly believe the Son of Man has stopped? Has the dwelling place of God stopped? If so, what is our promised land? Are we in it? How is it measured? What defines it? How is it recognized? Is it flowing with that which sustains life in a renewed society of love, justice, mercy, and humility? Or, is it plagued with the past? Though the koinonia consists of stones and pillars building up a spiritual house, these stones must be permitted to move and follow toward a destination if necessary. They should still obey. When they are together in unity, it is true koinonia. However, the moment we settle down, pitch our tents, build our structures, the wind blows and the footprints move. Then what? Do we have eyes to see and senses to feel such changes? Or, are we content to stay in our shop and anchored within our temporary tents?"

Ekklesia interjected, "You are being selfish. This journey is about you and your perspective. What about community? You are not meant to walk alone on this journey, and you are not meant to interpret such things alone. Be careful, Mathetes, that you do not turn the One into an 'individual god,' for the One is of an entire community and not just for you and your personal ambitions." Furthermore, Ekklesia said, "It is not your 'god' against my 'god' and neither is it your 'god' against ours." It was a cut to the heart. Could not the One be personal to me? I suppose I could understand Ekklesia's perspective, for I could imagine some have attempted to appease the One for personal gain at the expense of others.

These words, indeed, challenged me. Yes, we are not meant to walk this journey alone and there is wisdom and guidance in learning and teaching within a community. We are in need of community. Furthermore, there is great wisdom found in Ekklesia's exhortation. I would be wise to consider that the One is not for me personally and only me. Furthermore, it is not the One and me against all others. How can the One be for me only? Truly, the One is of an entire community and not just for me personally to have my bidding and to do my will and my agenda. I could easily be misled if I were to believe otherwise.

Perhaps it is a conditioning of my known world and context. That is, to be individualistic to the neglect of believing that the One is also of others as well. I thought it wise to pause and spend time in silence pondering these words. Furthermore, am I truly alone on this journey, as conveyed by Ekklesia?

While I am alone, I am not truly alone, for would it be possible that countless others have determined to be in such passionate pursuit as I am on this journey? Am I not in the company of the strength of those who have gone before me to show the way and demonstrate what it means to practice this space and discipline of following? Furthermore, this journey will teach me to not cater to the expectations of others, but rather, I am meant to truly discover who I am so that I might serve more effectively.

When I discerned fully the appropriate time, I responded. I said to Ekklesia, "Aspects of this journey might place me in a position of solitude and even quite possibly isolation, but I believe I will discover more intimately my source of strength. My journey will only lead to greater depths of spiritual health, for it will be based on my relationship in pursuit of the Son of Man rather than on my identity within the koinonia."

Ekklesia replied, "What about mission? As you follow, you still have an obligation to mission and to others. The Son of Man is devoted to mission. Therefore, you likewise have an obligation to follow the Son of Man into mission. On this isolated journey, you are serving no one but yourself."

I thought about these words for a moment. My internal dialogue began to wrestle with these thoughts. Indeed, there are two commands that stir up a flame inside of me. They are "follow me" and "go." I began to wonder if we can't have one without the other. I cannot fulfill mission until I have experienced what it truly means to follow.

Sensing the challenging nature of my friend, I ceased speaking. I needed to ponder and choose carefully my next words. "Ekklesia," I responded, "it appears that following the Son of Man for you is about a destination and a measurable outcome. As for me, following is about a discovery, and it's measured by the depths of transformation. Following is about remaining sensitive to the wind as it moves and shapes the koinonia. I believe following should precede mission. I would rather follow if it meant I would be more equipped to do mission.

My friend, I hope I have not offended you, and I hope I have not undermined your practices. My intent is not to speak ill of you, but I am going to continue in my pursuit. I truly believe I can be better equipped to serve only when I have truly learned how to follow. Can we find the perfect blend between you and me, or will our views be in constant tension? Can we unite? Imagine this: Ekklesia and Mathetes together. Imagine us on a journey together. Can we have both? Can we have both Ekklesia and Mathetes?"

Just then, Ekklesia said, "Mathetes, I intend to return to the village. That is where the people are and that is where our koinonia has settled. Furthermore, there we have a mission and that is where we have set up shop for the business of ministry. We must be there, for we have the teaching of the Son of Man. We must stay together."

As Ekklesia got up, I quickly replied, "But what about the movement? The footprints are moving. Can you not see them? The wind is blowing? Can you not feel it? How can we say we know the will of the One when I question if we truly reflect the image of the One? What have we to show from our journey and commitment to follow?" I continued, "We must keep going. As long as there are footprints, we must keep following. As long as the wind is blowing and beckoning us, we must keep moving." In that moment, I, Mathetes, invited Ekklesia to join me on this journey to follow the call of the wind and the footprints and to learn more through the created order about the One who created us. I said, "You have the words. You teach the words. You tell the stories. Come, follow with me on this journey."

Ekklesia turned back toward me and interjected with a defensive tone, "What about the words and the teachings? Mathetes, he has left this for us. I just don't understand what you're doing." I felt a deep tension between words carved on stone and the life I felt flowing from the journey of following the wind and the footprints. I realized that words on stones that never move are ineffective, but words in conjunction with a life-giving wind will flourish.

I stood up from the rock upon which I sat and said, "I know Ekklesia, and his words on stone and his teachings are my hope. They provide inspiration, and encouragement. While the words and teachings feed my soul, I will still follow."

Just then, I could see the look of disappointment on the face of Ekklesia. Fixing her eyes toward the ground she said, "Was I not able to help you on this journey? You are demanding perfection from me and you are demanding perfection from the koinonia. Neither I nor the koinonia is perfect. Why were we not enough for you?"

As I stepped closer to her, with softer words, I said, "No. I neither expect perfection from you nor the koinonia, but you are not the end of my journey. I do not believe the end of the journey is to arrive at the koinonia. On my journey, I'm not convinced that I was meant to merely find you as the end result of my journey. You are not my destination. You were meant to help me on my journey to know the One, find the Son of Man, and learn to follow for myself. Even though I am a part of the koinonia, you are only a shadow. You point me toward the substance."

Ekklesia looked up and said, "This journey will cost you. Others do not understand it. They will talk about you." I sighed as I acknowledged the truth of her words. I looked around at the silent landscape of the wasteland surrounding me and took a moment to contemplate. There was silence. I knew there was not much there to sustain any life. I was desperate to follow, and I wanted to be led away from that place in the wilderness. I broke the silence and said, "Ekklesia, one thing I have learned is this: the flowers spring up and return back to the earth. Let it be so with all within the palm of my hand. Upon the altar, I lay the memory of all that the One has done for me. I forsake where he has been. Learning from the past, I will follow where he goes until the journey comes to an end. I do not know the will of God, but maybe on this journey, I will discover it. By following the wind and seeking out the footprints, I will cling to the One. In this present moment, I know that I am meant to follow."

Then I said, "Goodbye, my friend, for there is more I want to learn and I intend to continue in my pursuit of the wind and the footprints." With these words, we turned from one another and parted ways. I watched as she walked into the distance and disappeared beneath the horizon.

I believed I would see Ekklesia again, but when I did, I would be transformed. I would be ready to offer myself to the koinonia in ways that I couldn't before my journey. I didn't want to pretend to be something I wasn't. I needed to offer myself to the only One who could change me and prepare me. Perhaps following the Son of Man will strengthen me to give back to both Ekklesia and the koinonia. While I held sound advice and instruction in high regard, I couldn't allow someone to tell me God's will, or what's more, God's will for me. I was afraid that others might disapprove of my journey, but I intended to follow. I began to discover how my journey was truly becoming about a process rather than a destination.

As I continued down the narrow path in a hot and dry barren land, for the first time, I truly felt lonely. The wind was gone. Or at least I couldn't feel it; the footprints were gone; Ekklesia thought I was foolish, and I was no longer basking in creation, but rather, the sun and the heat beat down on my head. Doubts began to creep to the surface. If ever I needed Ekklesia and the koinoinia, it was now.

I fell to my knees and prayed. My words failed me but my spirit cried out as if to say, "I do not have any strength to continue." From my heart, I began to sense my deepest desire within me. I resonated with others who had preceded me in retreating to the desert. As I allowed this space of solitude to shape me and form me, I cried in prayer, "Oh God, make me fit for my true place of service." I closed my eyes and was given a vision. In my vision, I was in a green field. The sun was shining and piercing through the clouds. It was a gorgeous day. I looked on top of a grassy hill and noticed a fruit tree. There was joy and laughter surrounding the tree. At the base of the tree, children were playing and adults were enjoying fellowship with one another. People were picking the fruit from the tree and enjoying its sweet taste. The juices from ripe fruit were sweet to the taste and satisfying for the appetites of the people. The tree was the center of this grassy hill and it was the source of joy for all. By this tree, there was pure rest, pure refreshment, and pure satisfaction.

Flowing from the tree was the fruit that brought life. It flowed from deep within. The roots were nourished by living water. The laughter and joy of this experience was nothing less than amazing.

Even with my physical eyes wide open, I could see this vision. What I could not see in the outward circumstances of the present moment, I saw within my spirit and soul. I suppose this is what it means to have a vision. Even when physical sight fails us and when we are discouraged by the reality of the present, we keep vision before us of what could be.

When one person's experience looks out on the landscape before me with weariness, another looks on with potential. When one person experiences challenges, another sees possibilities, and when one perspective succumbs to uncertainty, another sees opportunity. However, does one have the strength to make such an investment to cultivate what is needed for vision and possibilities? While the vision remains, it is both in the present and yet to come, but still one must wait. This is vision. Oh Lord, may I never lose sight of vision.

Regardless of what one measures in the present, there is something to come. This vision of the tree and its influence over all that it touched was beyond understanding. The tree reminded me of the central gathering point for a community of people who share in the common life. All of life is meant to be centered around the nourishment of the tree.

I have been convinced of what this has meant for all those who are on this journey. There is a space where the community gathers together, not necessarily physically but spiritually. It's possible for two lives to never meet and still to share this in common. It is the sharing of the centrality of the tree. Two souls that never once did meet are both at home in the presence of the tree. The tree has brought us together in community.

The tree has caused us to have dependency. We abide in the source of its nourishment, and we acknowledge the source of joy found at the tree. The tree is a space of safety. One might say to another: "Have you been there? Do you know the place of which I speak?" It is at the tree we find rest. It is at the tree we gather for joy and laughter. It is the tree that sustains. I have been convinced that those who understand the source of life at the center of this tree are blessed. Here is a profound reflection worth pondering. Is the tree found and discovered or does the tree have potential to be planted, rooted, and nurtured? Is the tree meant to thrive and flourish in the hearts and lives of those dedicated to making the tree its center?

As the wind has blown, without a doubt it is understood that seeds are blown. There are seeds constantly being blown from the very source of the life of this tree. A seed cultivated and nurtured within the appropriate environment reaches its fullest potential. It is evidence that when it appears that nothing is transpiring, if we listen to the wisdom of the seed, something is happening beneath the surface. As seeds scatter and take root, they will become life and fruit to those who notice, are aware, and are mindful to cultivate the process. The wind blows forcefully when needed and gently when necessary. The important aspect is the wind scatters these seeds and they sprout up to show evidence that there is an original tree; it has an original purpose; it possesses life and fruit to those with the wisdom and ability to find it, and it points to a way back to its Creator and puts the image of the One on display. Oh how refreshing it is to eat of this fruit and drink from the depths of living water flowing from this tree and from sprouted vegetation replicated from its seed! It is life and refreshment to those who abide in it. I saw this within my spirit, and I knew I could never be the same again.

With the vision still fresh in my mind, I began to pray, "Oh God, fill me with living water. I want to have a fruitful life." This vision showed me that fruit cannot be forced. It cannot be imitated. It is natural, cultivated, and grown.

"I am tired of 'doing,'" I cried. "Oh Lord, I want to be, so that by being, my work might flow from the depths of my innermost being." I wondered if others have also felt the striving I felt. Where would I possibly be without the source of all my strength? I have been convinced of my need. Also, I am expected to share with others what I have received. I cannot share that which I do not have. I simply cannot be what I am not.

I am discovering how I need to believe in the possibilities available for the one who trusts in our source of strength. There is a bit of irony embedded within this moment of reflection. The community gathered at the tree stands in contradiction to my words to Ekklesia. I asserted my position and demanded I continue on in this journey alone without the koinonia. Now, I have come face-to-face with my need to reconcile in these areas.

Of course, it is true that this journey is meant for me alone. It is my personal journey in pursuit of the Son of Man. The koinonia cannot do this for me. Also, in this moment and during this season, the koinonia is not with me. This has been my choice and my decision to wrestle with the lessons of my individual pursuit of drawing near to the heart of the One.

However, this one thing I have come to understand: if all of us in passionate pursuit centered ourselves together on our need to abide in the source and nourishment from the tree, then we would all be together in unity and on this journey toward the common destination in front of us.

I didn't enjoy the desert, but I understood the lessons it brought me. I learned to persevere and to keep going when it's hot. I learned to pause when I needed a rest, and my physical thirst motivated me to keep pursuing what I believed to be the only solution for my dry and weary soul.

Then suddenly, there it was! As I looked up, I saw a gorgeous sight. Streams of living water were flowing down the mountain into a lush green oasis. As I bent down to drink, I found footprints. It appeared that the Son of Man had stopped here to rest. I looked up and saw a cover of clouds rolling over an area that looked nothing like the desert. I knew it would be the location for the next part of my journey.

As I departed the barren wilderness, I found myself entering an entirely different landscape. I could see the scenery of my next journey in front of me. It appeared dark and cold, but I knew I needed to go through it.

V. Stuck

When I stepped into the swampy area of the next phase of my journey, I quickly sank. Mud enclosed my feet up to my knees. The stench of murky water reached my nostrils, and it made me want to vomit. "What is this place?!" I cried.

While walking through the swamp, I saw barren trees with dead leaves and broken branches. This appeared to be all that was left of this wasteland. My garments were stained with mud. I thought, "Why here? Where is the Son of Man going?"

I questioned the reason for my being in such a condition. Did I do something wrong? Did I take a wrong turn? Why was I here? Obviously, I thought this was a mistake. To be honest, maybe it was? Who is to say that our lives do not take twists and turns and we end up in places where we were never meant to be. It's interesting how I often hear the best of intentions from others suggesting that all of life is planned and there are never any mistakes. I suppose some might suggest this is a matter of destiny, however one understands and defines destiny. Are we destined to experience the things that happen to us? Or, are our entire lives up to us? In that moment, I believed that place was a mistake. I should not have been there and I refused to believe that was the place intended for me during that specific time of my life.

As I determined within myself that I was in the wrong place, I had to come to grips with the reality. I was there. I did end up there. Maybe we both were lost on this journey. Nevertheless, I would continue my journey forward. I wasn't supposed to be there at that time in my life, but I would look for the lessons and continue to inquire and ponder the deeper meaning of that place. I continued forward in that space.

Each step forward required more strength. I felt stuck. My muscles lacked the strength to continue. There were moments when I had to stop to cry. I wondered what Ekklesia would say if she could see me. Maybe she would tell me, "I told you so!" Or, "This is not God's will, so snap out of it and find strength in joy." But, I was reminded that the Son of Man also passed through this place. Perhaps Ekklesia would say it was all in my mind and that I could be released with enough faith. Or, it's possible that Ekklesia would tell me that either I or my ancestors had sinned and that's why I deserved this. I remembered the conversation I had with Ekklesia about being alone. Indeed, not only did I feel alone, but I felt incredibly lonely.

There was an undeniable loneliness within that space. On my journey, I did understand the need for company and community. While I traveled this path alone, I acknowledged the need placed in all of created humanity to not be alone and to have another on their journey. I began to also ponder my time in the koinonia. In hindsight, I began to wonder if there were visible signs of loneliness embedded within the individuals within that space of community. How can this be? Is it possible that one can be present and not be truly present? Is it possible that one can be in the company of another and still maintain a sense of unfulfillment and loneliness?

As it would seem, there must be a difference between being physically present and genuinely emotionally present. We are built to not only be in the presence of others but to have quality of presence with others. I cried out, "Oh Lord, I am lonely. While I believe that I have all I need and all I could ever want on this journey following you, my need for community has never been stronger."

Furthermore, I have come to realize that loneliness is a root of tension. When others feel uninvited or excluded, whether they realize it or not, it's the loneliness that is causing the reactionary behavior, and that loneliness generates a response. Therefore with this awareness, there is indeed better understanding concerning the root cause of loneliness.

As I reflected on all of these thoughts, it still was not clear why I was following within a swamp. The muddy swamp does something to your mind. It generates irrational fears and doubts. I didn't know I was capable of thinking such things. I was stuck, not only physically, but also spiritually and emotionally. I wondered what was grabbing me and hindering me from moving forward. Some of the mud was so thick I couldn't pass through it, so I had to go back the way I came and try another route. Inevitably, I felt like a failure.

Painful memories surfaced as I struggled through the swamp. With each memory, another stain appeared on my garment. I felt the power of the swamp, not only externally, but also internally. The swamp was my reality. I needed to get to the root cause of this paralysis. It kept me stuck. Taking steps forward involved being honest with my past and brokenness. No one ever said coming face-to-face with the past was going to be easy. I reminded myself repeatedly that God is near to the brokenhearted and God comforts my crushed spirit.

I wondered why Ekklesia and the koinonia never taught me about the swamp. Could they have helped me prepare for this experience? Perhaps they didn't know it existed, or perhaps they refused to talk about it. Nevertheless, the swamp surrounds me and I have no choice but to face it. However, this place doesn't just appear. It was familiar, as if it had always been present with me, but I was too busy and too inattentive to notice. Now, here I was without a choice. The path forward was through the swamp.

I could see the edge of the swamp, but I could not fly over it. How I wish I could soar above this experience. The only way out of this was to walk through it. Every wrong turn brought a new perspective. It was a test of my patience. The swamp was drawing out the worst in me. I was angry; I was stained and I was disgusted. I thought to myself, "How am I even fit to keep following the Son of Man? He will take one look at my stains and surely reject me." As a matter of fact, anyone would look at these stains with disgust, even the koinonia and Ekklesia. I realized that I could no longer bury my stains, my pain, and my shame, for these experiences always find a way to the surface. I realized that while I was physically stuck, my mind had been running. Why was I running?

There is a juxtaposition between being stuck and running away from something. The lesson is I neglected to face the strongholds buried deep within me. The pain has caused me to run away rather than face my problems. Running away from unhealed pain will only strengthen the power of the mud. Finally, I acknowledged the existence of that place. I was stuck in the depths of the unhealed wounds in my life that were buried deep within.

I could not deny the reality that as a part of this journey I had come to a space of unsettledness and irreconciliation. I allowed myself to settle into this experience further and replay the visions in my mind. What was causing this? Was it the things I have said? Was it the pain my words have caused others? It is interesting how the pain of my words to others came back to haunt me. It is interesting how the things I have said to cause others pain cling to me as a weight of thickness. This weight of thickness is pulling me deeper and deeper into the mud. It is not only the words I have said, but there are things I have done.

I began to realize the deeds I have done with deep regret. How was I to know better? Oh Lord, how was I to know that my deeds of the past would plant seeds of guilt and would give rise to flourishing regret and shame? I have done things of which I am not proud. I thought they were done and over with, and I am realizing they are not gone. They have returned with paralyzing consequences.

Then, I considered my omissions. What should I have done that I didn't do? Where did I fail to act? If I could go back, I would say, "I'm sorry," to the ones I have hurt, or I would sit over a meal and listen to the ones whom I failed. Maybe I was not present when I needed to be? In this, I was stuck. Could I go back? It is commendable to the one willing to go back and say, "I'm sorry." That is to say, "Forgive me. I'm not that person anymore."

How I wish I could go back to those spaces to say I am no longer that person. But then came the doubt. The mud was keeping me in a place of believing that something had been present with me. "Oh my God, now I see myself. Let me see myself how you want to see me. There is no life here in the swamp."

While I needed to come face-to-face with my past, there is no life dwelling in the shame and regret of the past. It is like a scar that has opened up once again as a wound, and perhaps after this experience it will remain as a scar—meaning, the memory exists within my vision, but the wound no longer has power over my present. I chose to not deny the swamp, but to pursue life and to no longer allow it to have power over me.

As I contemplated the rut of my past, I came face-to-face with it. I was forgiven, but somehow I still saw the person I had hurt in my mind before me. It was a paralysis to my progress. I wept for the past, but I longed for the strength to weaken its grip on my present. I wept for the past, but I maintained hope for the future. I did so in the strength that the past no longer had a grip on me. However, this seemed to be a recurring struggle. My only hope was my strength would continue to be strengthened.

I surrendered. I surrendered not to shame, guilt, and regret, because deep inside, though I was still learning about the Son of Man, I didn't believe that was where I was meant to stay and dwell. However, I believed I was meant to face the struggle I encountered there, not to give power over to that place, but rather to acknowledge and even respect its potential to paralyze us on our journey.

I have found it interesting to consider this one thing from this experience. In my pursuit of the Son of Man, and in my journey to move away from where I once was following him, somehow, it led me back here. In pursuing and following, it didn't mean I denied where I once had been. Maybe I was meant to be the person I was becoming in the context of my past without being of my past. I no longer could deny that place. It was a part of who I once was and a part of the story of my very journey in pursuit of footprints. There was nothing I could do in my own strength.

Rather, I surrendered to my helplessness. I surrendered to my inability to do anything within my own power and strength to pull myself out of this.

Somehow, my mind shifted to a practical solution: "I cannot go back, but in going forward, I can remember where I have been. I can be a voice from the past to the generation yet to come. I know I can begin changing the future here in the present. The echoes of the past cry out for wisdom in the present in such a way as to influence the very trajectory of the future."

What would it be? When I completed this journey, would I make decisions to come alongside the very path of someone else and guide their journey with wisdom, urging others not to repeat the same mistakes of the generations before them? It is indeed a truth that others need to take responsibility for their own actions, but I dare not stand idle on the sidelines and watch. While this practical voice of wisdom was like a calling and a stirring action inside of me, I needed to come face-to-face with my inability to get out of the mirky swamp. My mind came back to the reality of my present situation. How can I help others when I cannot even help myself? Who am I to believe I am the voice of wisdom when I am stuck? Who am I to believe I can be a voice for others when I myself have once been there? Hypocrite, I am? Perhaps. Or I am an example. Learn from me on your journey. As I attempt to be sensitive to the needs of the next generation, I declare, "My children, learn and pay attention. Exercise wisdom and sound judgment for life."

In my swamp, in the very lowest moment I could have possibly been in, I knew my deepest need and knew I was incapable of pulling myself out by my own strength. Rather than striving to be released, I prayed, "Oh Lord, my God, out of these depths I cry to you. Bring washing, cleansing, and healing from the depths of who you are."

As I came to this realization, I noticed the changing landscape. The change wasn't immediate. Gradually, the ground beneath my feet dried up, and I noticed tiny green blossoms on the trees, as if the season of spring had arrived after a long, cold, dark winter.

I could see a little freshwater stream flowing and washing away the stale and stagnant water. The stench of dead vegetation was replaced by the scent of a fresh and lush forest. I heard birds chirping in the branches and I saw chipmunks hurrying up the trees ready to devour their food. Soon it became clear that I had reached the end of the swamp. It was gone but not forgotten. Maybe it will appear again? Who knows? On this phase of my journey, I came to the edge of a timberline. I was standing at the foot of a beautiful mountain range.

As I looked back to the space of the swamp, I wondered what it would be like to return, and if I would ever go back. It began to dawn on me that the swamp has strongholds on me when I empower it.

VI. Helpless

When I came to the foot of the mountains, I felt lost and confused. The vegetation of the mountain forest was thick and dense. I couldn't see beyond the layers of branches, leaves, and ferns. I was overwhelmed by the sight of so many trails. I was not certain which path I needed to take. I fell to my knees and wept, and again, I cried out in prayer.

As I opened my eyes, there they were! The footprints! I couldn't see them while standing, but with my face humbly and lowly in the dirt, I could see clearly. I continued on with my journey with confidence and assurance in the direction in which I was headed. I was in pursuit of the footprints.

I ventured through a trail of switchbacks and ascended higher and higher through the dense timberline. To my amazement, the forest was beginning to teach me some of life's greatest lessons.

I stumbled upon an old tree that had fallen in the forest. Initially, my first impression was to complain about this tree. It was in my way. On this journey, I have come face to face with this barrier and a very frustrating one at that. As I climbed to the top of it, I decided to rest upon it. Just then I began to look around and take in the scenery. While the forest was dense with cedar trees and thick ferns, I could see light poking through the pockets of space in between the branches and needles high above my head.

As I looked toward the heavens, I could see the clouds moving and being blown by the wind. Once again, there was the wind on my journey as a teacher. It swayed the branches back and forth and the smaller trees from side-to-side. It was gentle in that moment, but I knew the wind has the power to destroy. When the wind is unleashed, it has the power to bring destruction. Can anyone contain the wind? Only the wind contains itself. Only the wind knows where to go and the force of its own strength.

In that moment, while sitting in the presence of the forest, I could hear the wind. How amazing to consider the very fact that wind produces a noise and I have never been still enough to notice. It is known only to those and by those who have the ears to listen to its sound. There were a few birds chirping off in the distance, but other than that, there was complete silence. As I listened to the wind, I could hear the leaves rustling. It was a combination of wind and rustling. This moment had become my teacher on this journey once again.

My prayer began to be that I would find the space and the stillness to allow me to hear the still small voice of the wind when it wants to speak. However, I am aware that the conditions need to be right. In that space, I didn't hear the sound of the hustle and bustle as I would in the marketplace. However, I found it fascinating that even in such a space as the marketplace, the mysterious Son of Man found me and beckoned me, but yet I was called out and invited to the space of the present moment.

While sitting upon the tree I wondered what had caused it to lose strength enough to be uprooted, causing it to tumble to its final resting place on the forest floor. There was no life left it in, yet interestingly enough it had a purpose. In the same way, is it not interesting how we can learn so much from the echoes of the past? The written record of those who have gone before us still speaks to us today. What does it say? Perhaps it is a memoir to a great legacy. The once strong and solid tree stood high and held up its strength by the nurture within its roots.

With the pride of our height, there is often the danger of a fall, for we are not intended to live forever. On the other hand, it's not about being proud of our height and strength at all. We are intended to be present in our time, to serve our purpose, and then one day to leave it to the next generation; so it is with this mighty tree that once stood tall and no longer is, but what is its legacy? I jumped to my feet to admire the width and thickness testifying to its age and strength. While walking along the tree, I came across something beautiful and almost indescribable. There was a little tree taking root and sprouting up. It only came to my knees in height, but I captured a glimpse of its resilience.

As I gazed at the tree, a light shining through the thickness of the forest hovered over the dead tree and rested on the new life sprouting from the remnants of the old tree. I could see a few branches and leaves growing. This tree was on its way. It wasn't planted on the ground. It was growing out of the nurture and remains of the old tree. It was pushing itself and demanding for there to be new life and rebirth. If the old tree had not died, the new life would not have been born.

This is it! It's amazing when it all makes sense. When one gives oneself in this great act of selfless love, there is life renewal and opportunity for others. I get it. There is another lesson to the tree, and it's not as pleasant to ponder.

What if something living has run its course and time and now it has given itself up in order for something else to take its space? This is not as pleasant to consider, and yet I think about weeds growing up with the fruit and nourishment of the garden. I consider the space occupied by weeds and believe that these often need to be uprooted for new life to thrive and flourish in that space. How patient must the gardener be to allow the unfruitful vegetation to run its course and time prior to harvesting fruit.

When will it be required of me to graciously set aside myself for something new to thrive and flourish in my place? What will it be like? Will I resist this in pride? Will I clench my fist around my position, and will I be overcome with pride? I don't want to die one day and I don't want to be too old to be useful.

It's the way of all things. Oh Lord, find me faithful in my time, and give me wisdom and discernment to know when it's time to lay myself aside to provide the space required and needed for new life to sprout up and for new life to thrive and flourish. Bring renewal with the touch of your hand.

My only prayer is this: help me to not give up and quit. I don't want to easily surrender my life when it is time to persevere. I don't want to quit when I must cling to my faith and continue on the journey with endurance. Oh Lord, grant me wisdom to discern this.

This was one of the more profound spiritual moments on my journey. This image spoke to me about the way of life, spirituality, and the inevitable cycles of life. All of it is in the hands of the One in whom I am in passionate pursuit. The spiritual moment began to fade and I began to grow uneasy. While the forest was calm and peaceful, my thoughts started to turn to a sense of restless anxiety.

I thought about the dangers of the forest. The worries and fears of the forest were different from the swamp and rugged terrain of the desert. I thought, "Where am I going? And what is beyond the trees?" I felt vulnerable. Ascending into the mountains, and pushing my way through a trail of timber, I realized how much I did not want to be there. I was filled with fear.

My internal fears were being projected onto the environment around me. I did not know if my fear of the environment was from outside or from within, but I knew I needed to face my fears. The only way to overcome this experience was to go through it.

Why now? Why should fear show up in this space and come and go as it pleases just like an uninvited guest? Fear is one of the most powerful forces in existence. In some ways, it can keep us vigilant and cautious. In other words, fear teaches us to guard against blindly putting our faith and confidence in people and places that do not have our best interest at heart.

Then, I suppose, there is unhealthy fear. That is the fear that has taken root and has flourished in a space within those who don't have confidence or a high self-esteem. It resides within those who have been betrayed by others and the fear enables them to set a guard over the heart. In this space, I must continue to face my deepest fear and replace it with a sense of self-worth. I hear the voice of fear, and I listen for it. I respect the precautions for me to avoid dangers and risks, yet where fear is due to a lack of self-confidence and self-worth, I must challenge its power over me and keep moving forward.

As I began to ascend a hill, the temperature dropped, and the altitude increased. I was freezing and helplessly exposed to the mercy of the elements. The air was cold and crisp. Snow flurries began to drizzle. Thousands of tiny little flakes were floating and resting on the green timberline. It was a beautiful sight. I came to the top of a peak overlooking a valley. I could see miles of snow-capped mountains. The wind blew over my face as I gazed upon the pure white freshness of the snow. For a moment, I rested to breathe in life and to enjoy the beauty all around me. I looked for the footprints, and I didn't see them. However, I knew the one whom I was following. I started to wonder if he also stopped for a moment to take in this beauty. Had he stopped long enough to breathe in the indescribable majesty of creation before our very eyes? My conditioned busy lifestyle and busy mind both told me, "No." My way of interpreting the Son of Man and the world around me had instilled a sense of "urgency" deep within. "Keep going," I thought to myself, "as there is so much to do." How foolish are these thoughts and how foolish of me to project this onto the Son of Man. I wept because all my life I believed this to be true. I had to fight this. I needed to be honest. I had always believed that God accepts me because I have a sense of urgency to perform works. I was sad. While standing on the top of this peak, I was soaking in the beauty of creation, and I reminded myself that even the Son of Man would have stopped to enjoy the beauty all around me. Why can't I allow myself to rest and believe that with such an act God would still be pleased with me? This is creation. This is the product of my Creator. Then there was silence. I sat in silence. I could hear the gentle blowing of the wind through the valley below. All else was silent before the Creator. It was peaceful. After a few hours, I decided to keep moving.

As I continued, suddenly, the frailty of my human body became evident. I was weary and cold. The beauty of the snow brought with it a strenuous walk, and as I stopped to rest, I felt discomfort. The freezing temperature caused my whole body to shiver. I was wrestling with tension. I said to myself, "How could a place of such beauty bring with it such discomfort?" My vulnerability and sensitivity to the cold could no longer be hidden. I realized that my body needed necessities. I needed shelter. I needed a roof over my head. I needed protection from the elements. The reality of my created human body was speaking to me.

The snowfall began to increase with intensity, and as I focused my eyes to pierce beyond the wall of white snow before me, I saw what appeared to be an old cabin in the distance. It was small but inviting. I made my way toward the cabin. It was made of timber logs. I entered slowly through the door. It was cold but there was evidence of a human presence. I looked around at all the cobwebs and dust within the cabin. I managed to find a few matches and some wood and paper tucked deep within the corner of an area. There was a small furnace. It was nothing less than a miracle. I thought, "Why is this here? How can this be possible?" I was so filled with joy that tears began to flow from my eyes at this provision. I couldn't believe it. I quickly cleared the old furnace and stuffed it with fresh wood and paper. I was careful not to waste one single precious match. I struck the match and protected the flame by cupping my hands over the match the way a mother would protect an infant in her arms. Life was precious and this flame was the secret to sustaining my life in this very moment. As the paper and wood began to kindle a flame, I carefully blew on the flame to increase its power. Ironically, this caused me to consider how the wind, a very breath itself, was ever present and with me on this journey. The wind provided strength during times of need. It reminded me to pray for the fanning of the flame in my life through the very breath that could only come from the One. I felt the warmth of the fire and it brought comfort. I began to consider all the simple things in life I had taken for granted. It could be summed in one simple word, "gratitude." I could no longer take anything for granted.

Somehow, the snow and the temperature reminded me of my need to be grateful. I was thankful for clothing, the warmth of a fire, and all the provisions that could only come from my Creator.

Indeed, I was grateful for times of warmth and comfort. I want to be thankful every day for provision. My basic need for warmth was being restored, and I rested with relief. Then, there was silence.

As the fire lit up the dark room, I could both sense its warmth and see more clearly. As I walked around the cabin, I began to soak in the story all around me. There was an echo of the past within those walls. There was a silent story longing to be shared.

As I explored the cabin, I realized there wasn't much there. It was seasonal and it has surrendered to a new beginning, but why? Who was here? What did they do while they were here? Were they hunters? Or were they mining for gold? As curious as I was, I realized that it didn't matter. It dawned on me: Whoever was here was selflessly mindful of the future. Whoever was here had consideration for a weary traveler such as myself to one day arrive. Whoever was here knew that one day I would come here, and I would be in need. Whoever it was prepared this place for me to be here in this very specific time in history. Is this not an aspect of our journey of faith? That is, to prepare the path for those to follow? The miracle of my shelter happened because someone thought about me prior to knowing me. Someone, who didn't even know my name, prepared this place for my arrival. Is this not the characteristic of our Creator? There is a finite element to humankind. We spend our time building something for ourselves in the present only to leave it to a generation yet to come. All of our accomplishments and achievements, when built on the wrong foundation and for the wrong motives, will one day turn to dust. This is an important perspective to remember. On this journey, the Creator used the creation to provide for me. How blessed I was to be helped by strangers. This challenged me. It begged me to ponder this question: What am I doing in the present for someone in the future? Why would it matter? God had used someone in the past to meet my need in the present. To me, that's beautiful. "Use me, God!" This became my prayer. I had nothing to leave behind except for a few matches, some paper, and wood. I wanted to keep the blessing moving forward for those who were yet to come. Indeed, I have all I need.

There is something about a warm fire that is soothing and relaxing. Placing your hands out over the flame and absorbing the heat in comfort has a therapeutic effect. The warmth of a fire coupled with a relaxing ambience has been the birthplace of some of the most profound conversations centered around the work of the soul.

Sitting around the warmth of a fire, a group of men and women engage in conversations and find the space ideal for catering to vulnerability. The fire can be a window into the soul. While gazing on its beauty, a group of friends are willing to share the deepest and most vulnerable conversations. They share about ambitions in life, twists, turns and struggles. I have learned a lot about myself through processing my thoughts next to a fire.

The fire creates the space for listening. From the dear friend who is invited to slow down through the relaxation of the fire and share his or her story, we should listen attentively and allow others to share. I want to be fire for someone else. I want to be that presence of warmth, comfort, and assurance, and I want to be a space of hospitality. Is this not a depiction of our Creator, and the One whom I am passionately pursuing? It is within the stories.

As Ekklesia would share about the Son, she would explain how his acts of hospitality have invited others to feel welcomed and accepted in his presence. When one feels the space of hospitality, love, assurance, and acceptance, it's easy to share and to be vulnerable. The invitation has been extended. Come. Sit. Share. Be in the presence. Bask in the warmth and comfort of the fire.

While the soothing and relaxing ambience of the fire brought warmth and peace to my soul, I began to come face-to-face with the juxtaposition of the fire. Too close to it, and you'll burn. If you let it get out of control, it becomes a raging danger, and when not contained, the fire has the potential to bring destruction. The koinonia and Ekklesia speak of fire as an image teaching us the very lessons of the mystery of the One whom I am devoting my heart to pursue.

This fire has the potential to consume and yet it is restrained. This fire has the potential to bring hurt and destruction and yet it is controlled and tamed. The one who has the greatest power with fire must exercise responsibility. This caused me to realize that I had been given a great responsibility, and I could use it for good or use it for destruction. My prayer in that moment was that I would be like the One who has strength and yet does not wrongfully consume; but may what is wrong be consumed by fire.

The fire purifies. The fire burns out what needs to be burned up so that the purities remain. The fire burns up the old and yet brings forth new life and renewal. In such a way, my soul, oh my soul, learn from the fire. Study its image. May it be used for good and purity. My lesson from that moment was to be responsible with that which has been entrusted to me.

After putting out the fire, I departed from the warmth of the cabin. I knew I couldn't remain there forever. I needed to continue this pilgrimage. I had not yet arrived at the end of my journey. I left a bundle of wood, some matches, and paper for the next person who might one day follow me and arrive at this place on a journey.

As I kept moving, the sun started to pierce the clouds. The brightness shone over the white and green landscape. Off in the distance, I could see a stream flowing. It was flowing downward. As I watched the snow melt away, I thought how beautiful it was to know that winter seasons do not last forever, and, in time, even the cold will yield to the warmth of the sun. In time, the dark winter will cease in preparation for the arrival of the blossoms of spring. As the sun shone and warmed by face and body, I kept walking. Then, there was silence.

VII. Through Living Waters

There was a flowing stream just off in the distance and it fed a waterfall rushing down the side of a mountain. It plummeted with full force into a pool of water below. The lush green vegetation, coupled with the sound of the rushing water, was soothing. This was a perfect spot to take a rest. I knelt down to wash my muddy face, and that's when I noticed my reflection. Something was different about me, for I could barely recognize myself. Written on my face, I could see struggle mingled with transformation. There was a sense of exhaustion mixed with anticipation. This experience was visibly known through the signs on my face. I was marked by my journey. My face was sunburnt from walking in the wilderness. My hair was filled with sand; my lips were cracked from the dry and bitter cold. I was pushed beyond my comfort zone, but still I felt different. Despite the marks and scars from my journey, I felt a renewed sense of meaning and purpose.

Kneeling at the pool of water and staring at my reflection gave me a new lesson. That is, my reflection keeps me from seeing underneath the surface of the water. I wondered how often I had allowed myself to get in the way of recognizing the work beneath my layers? I pondered the past, and how I would take too much time worrying about my appearance. Or, how I could easily worry about what others think. I was plagued with people-pleasing because I was too worried about keeping up with appearances. Because of this, I would often neglect to look beneath the surface and peer into the internal world. That is where the true work of transformation is found. These are the areas that God wants to penetrate.

During this phase of my journey, I was beginning to grasp the truth that there is One who truly knows me deep inside, and the wind has searched the depths of my innermost being. I was coming to the realization that this was an internal journey. When the Son of Man said, "Follow me," the depth of these words transcended far beyond a mere physical location. The words "follow me" have invited me to participate on a journey of discovery to unveil the design of the unique individual whom I was created to be. "Follow me," says the Son of Man. Then he leads us on a journey to discover where we are, who we are, how we are, and why we are. With the depth of this realization, I cried out, "Oh God, thank you for your work of transformation." Then, I was silent.

After my brief rest, I lifted my eyes to become familiar with my surroundings. I saw that there was no possible way to go around the stream, and surely I could not go back the same way I came. The footprints were gone, and I didn't see the Son of Man, so I passed through the stream. The water was cool and refreshing. It cleansed me, and it washed my swamp-stained garments. However, the memory of the swamp was still present. How could I easily forget such an experience? After my journey through the rugged wilderness, I could not take this lush refreshment for granted, and I could not forget the heat of the desert. These experiences would remain with me forever as a part of my story.

I drew nearer to the other side of the stream. I knew I was close to my destination, and I was filled with great anticipation. I wondered, "What will be my reward for my faithfulness on this journey? Perhaps there's money and gold, or I might find a stone with my name written on it. Maybe I will be dubbed the 'greatest servant of all' and I will bask at the right hand of the Son of Man." With this anticipation, I shouted, "I must be the greatest!" The echo traveled down through the canyon and bounced off the rocks. As the echoes reached my ears, the thought of my greatness was inflated. Little did I realize the leaven of pride that was rising up within my own heart and mind, and I would soon be humbled once again. When I came to the end of the stream, I looked up to see a waterfall flowing from a crevice at the top of a vertical wall of rock. I couldn't believe it. My self-exaltation had receded and succumbed to the reality that was before me. I was downcast and disappointed. My joy vanished. I persevered through this entire journey to end at a sheer rock wall with simply no possible way to climb it.

All of my excitement about my achievements and accomplishments were shattered. I simply could not climb this. I sat down and wept. I was questioning my decision. I was questioning why I was here. I couldn't scale this rock, and I didn't even know what was at the top of the surface above me. Even now, at the end of the journey, I had to figure out how to overcome this impossible task before me. I sat in silence.

As I mustered up my strength, I decided to try and climb the wall. I had come so far and I didn't intend to fail. I reached for any possible spot where I could grip the rock with my hands. I felt the strain on my fingertips as I pulled my weight up with all my strength. I couldn't find a foothold on the surface of the slippery rock. I wanted to climb this wall, but I simply could not do so. There was nothing more I could do.

Just then, while I was weak and utterly helpless, I cried out for help. I knew the Son of Man had passed through this space and was now the only one capable of helping me. Just then, a hand reached out to grab me. I saw a gash on the hand and a bloodstain on the skin, as if the hand had been cut on these very rocks. I grabbed the hand and I felt myself being pulled up to the top of the ledge. I sat at the top to catch my breath for a moment. I looked around to familiarize myself with the surroundings of this new place.

The fog was thick, and a strong wind was blowing. Then, I saw another stream. It was the source of the waterfall. No gold; no reward; no riches; no trophies; no money; no success; no honor and no great name for myself. There before me was nothing but water. At first, I felt disappointed. I tasted the water. It was refreshing and satisfying. My weary journey made me yearn for such water.

I stood there and stared for a while. The water was gushing up like a fountain as it fed the lake surrounding it. This water had no beginning and no end. This was my reward. My reward was to be in the presence of the source of this water. I could not describe the beauty of the fountain in front of me. It made me speechless. To the one who takes such things for granted, he or she would not understand, but to the one who discerns such a gift, it's truly a source of healing and refreshment. I needed nothing else. Not gold, rewards, trophies, praise, recognition, and success; I simply needed living water flowing from a pure source. The pursuit of all else is meaningless.

I felt the wind blow across my face, and then the hand that pulled me up was placed upon my shoulder. I turned and looked to see the fog roll back, unveiling the face of the Son of Man standing there. In that moment, there were no words exchanged. I was struck with wonder.

Gazing on the Son of Man, I was aware that there was something different about his appearance. It wasn't the same as when I had seen him in the marketplace when I first began my journey. It was different. The interesting aspect is I wondered if he had changed or if I had changed—meaning, had his appearance been veiled to me and now I had the eyes and ability to see him differently?

Perhaps I needed eyes to see differently, and this journey had made this possible. I wondered, what purpose was there for enduring such a journey? How could I possibly tell this story to others? Do others have the capacity to be excited about the end results? This journey yields a fountain of living water as its reward. Would that be enough to persuade others to follow? There was beauty in the silence. As I humbled myself before the Son of Man, we were both silent. Words were not necessary for that moment. Silence was within the space, and I resided there with the One, the Wind and the Son of Man. In that moment, I surrendered to the silence; I trusted in the work of silence. I ceased and surrendered the space to the One greater than I.

After a time, I heard the voice of the Son of Man; the One whom I had been following. It was beautiful, for he spoke tenderly. It was not like the man I had heard in the village. It was not mysterious; the voice was familiar. I felt different in his presence, and by the appearance on his face, I found affirmation, courage, and perseverance.

I allowed myself time to reflect on my journey. I had learned to revisit my past and find healing for the future. I was familiar with stains and feelings of uselessness. I knew the feeling of being stuck in the mud of pain. I had learned to be washed and accepted. I learned to appreciate the cycles of life and to seek to live life with purpose during the few short years I'll have on this earth. I had learned to reach out and take the hand of the Son of Man. To my physical body, finding water was like finding the very source of life. In the same way, only the Son of Man was able to provide for my dry and thirsty soul.

VIII. Purpose

In this moment, I was granted an opportunity discovered by those who truly seek and who seek to follow wholeheartedly, for I was sitting in the presence of the Son of Man. It was different than the village. In the village, we know of the one, but is he known? It is possible to listen to words and spend time with someone and still have so much to learn.

Now, I am here and ready to take in these words in such a way that the power of the words will bring forth the fruit and transformation to be realized. One lingering question is this: Who does the Son of Man want me to become?

When the Son of Man spoke, I heard him say, "Grace and peace to you." Then there was silence again. Words could not add or take away from the feeling of that sacred moment. After a time of silence, the Son of Man said, "Mathetes, you are learning my ways not because you are merely a doer but because you are a follower."

I said, "Lord, I was lonely. I thought I had lost you. I didn't know where you were." Many times on this journey I was surrounded by chaos without a sense of peace and hope. How does all this make sense? I'm not sure there is an answer. I longed for the opportunity to be in the glorious presence to ask such questions, and even now, I don't know if there is an answer.

I must admit, there is something comforting about asking such questions. What if we find ourselves in the presence of the One who holds all the mysteries and the questions to all of life?

What if we could sit with the One to whom we have longed and desired to express our deepest questions and anxieties? What would we say? What would we ask? What would we hear in response? The comfort is not necessarily in the answers, but rather, the comfort seems to be in the opportunity and in the presence.

Often, by faith, we must believe there is someone holding all these things in place and operating for a greater purpose. The question to further ponder is this: Does our journey require complete understanding or quality of presence? Once again, I ask: How does all this make sense?

He said, "Be still, for here I am with you."

I replied, "What is your will for me and what am I to do? Some might suggest it's enough to memorize and recite your words and teachings and tell others to do the same."

He replied, "Know me. Do you know me? I know you. I saw you take my teaching and apply it to your life. I saw you follow me from the village to the wilderness. I saw you push through the storm and the desert. You were lonely but not alone. I know your struggles because I was there too. I saw you when you stained your garments with mud and dirt as you faced the pain of your past. You must find forgiveness in your heart, Mathetes. You must forgive yourself even as I have forgiven you. You must forgive those who have hurt you, betrayed you, said things about you that are untrue. You must listen to one voice and the only voice that matters. You must release yourself from the bondage of the things that have been done to you. You must forgive yourself for the pain you have caused others. Learn from it, receive my rest and forgiveness, for that is the only way forward. I saw you on your journey, and I still see you in this, my dear child."

He continued, "I saw you on your knees searching for my footprints. I saw you pass through the water to find rest and refreshment for your weary and thirsty soul. I saw you arrive at the freshness of the fountain of living water. When I reached out for your hand, it was then that you no longer merely looked for me, but you knew me and found me because you pursued me with your whole heart. I was with you when you found your reward.

What did you find? Gold? A crown? Trophies? An endless pursuit of temporal materials? No, my ways are beyond this, for there is only one thing that truly satisfies. At my source is an everlasting and ever flowing spring of cool and refreshing water, and there is a tree that is life to those who make such discoveries. Let it be so that others would answer the call. It is not a call to gain. It is not a call to benefit. It is not a call to obtain or to even achieve any agenda, but it is a call to a way of life. It is a call to lay down pride and choose to follow. It is a response to the invitation, 'follow me,' and you will know my ways. 'Follow me,' for though words can be taught, other lessons can only be caught. Remember this. Remember what I have told you. Remember what your eyes have seen. Remember where you have been. Remember my faithfulness on this journey. May others see the testimony and fruit of your devotion, marked not by deeds alone, but rather marked by a genuine pursuit of the One. May you be unto others fruit and living water, and may you draw others to the Son of Man. Come, Mathetes, keep following me, and I will show you more, for that is your purpose. That is my will for you and that is your deepest hunger and thirst. Follow me."

There was silence once again, for words failed me as I pondered what was spoken by my Lord.

We sat in stillness for quite some time. No words were exchanged, but I was not alone. I pondered the reflection of the seed from the tree within my vision, and I knew that there is also fruit to be discovered within the silence. While it seems nothing is happening, remember the seeds, and even in the space of the silence, something is stirring and rising up beneath the layers of the surface. As we sat together, I allowed these words to become my meditation and I reflected on their meaning. How do I move such words to practice within my life?

Even so, I longed for these words to become reality in both my life and in the lives of all who hear about the Son of Man. I began to wonder about the others whom I witnessed early on in this journey. I saw others pitching tents, tightening ropes, hammering stakes, and opening up for business to teach the words of this One whom I feel is hardly known to them. Who am I to judge?

May it not be so that I judge. However, as for my personal journey, I needed to further pursue. I needed to further contemplate, and I needed to further know this One. These things are worthy of reflection.

Furthermore, I was attempting to question at what point could I claim my soul was eternally right through the Son of Man, thus obtaining eternal security when I depart from the space of the living? Perhaps it was when the hand reached out and grabbed me? After all, one's soul cannot be saved until it acknowledges a need and therefore a willingness to receive that which we cannot do by ourselves and within our own abilities.

Or, could it be that at the moment I chose to follow, though I didn't understand all that would mean, it was at that point I put my trust in the Son of Man, by faith. As a result, my soul was well and prepared for all eternity.

Receiving a cleansed and purified soul is only the beginning of a journey that beckons us to follow.

I cannot cease to believe that there will ever come a time on my journey, regardless of the state of my soul, when I will ever have to cease trusting or when I will ever cease from following and pursuing the Son of Man, even if I am led by the footprints. Indeed, I put my trust in him, past, present, and future. I can imagine the individual sitting in the koinonia asking such a question with deep restlessness and uncertainty: "But Mathetes, at what point was your soul secured?" I suppose the best way for me to answer this question is with the negative. At what point might my soul be in danger? My answer is as follows: I suppose it would be the moment I cease to trust.

If my friend Ekklesia were here, we could continue to analyze this conversation through the words and teachings of the Son of Man, and I would also attempt to provide further explanations based on my experiences on this journey. Is there an element of faith required to be exercised while the soul is at peace and rest with the One? Yes, yes there is. Are there moments of doubt and uncertainty after our soul is at peace and rest with the One? Yes, yes there are. The moment I believe I could scale the sheer face of the rock cliff against the plummeting waters from the waterfall by myself and without the help of the Son of Man is when I believe that I am fully capable of putting my soul at peace with the One on my own and without any help.

This space is a dangerous space to be. My soul, from the moment I chose to trust, and especially, in the moment I received help knowing I was helpless, is the moment my humility demonstrated I needed to repent of all of my self-reliance and self-confidence, and as I continue down this path and journey of discovery, and as I continue to call out for the only one worthy and capable of making my soul at peace with the One, then it is well.

At the end of the journey, I began to focus on others. I would desire that all would answer such a call to follow, and I would wish for all to understand what this means. Indeed, it is a blessing and worthy of rejoicing to realize that there are those who have chosen to believe. To those who have chosen to believe, I want to encourage you to continue to follow. Reflecting on my journey, I realized that by following, we obey the commission to "go." By following, we attract others to follow. As we keep our eyes on the footprints, and as we respond to the movement of the wind, we better understand ourselves and we better understand our mission and our purpose.

Our deepest desire and our relentless pursuit should be to understand our purpose and our great design. In this discovery, we die to who we are not and we cultivate the soil to become who we were created to be. At the end of this journey, I understood more than ever what it means to "die to self."

I began to realize that I never fully understood this. "Dying to self" didn't necessarily mean to forget who I am and be conformed to the expectations of others. Are we meant to follow people's expectations or are we meant to faithfully obey and follow the footprints before us?

This journey has taught me profound lessons, and I would desire to encourage others who choose to follow. I would tell them to keep going, even when the footprints seem to disappear. The movement of the wind is the unseen encouragement that compels us to move forward. We feel it; we sense it; we try to grasp it. However, we can only respond.

Truly the wind was the source used to stir a fire deep within my soul. Where would I be without this? My soul's burning passion was set ablaze by the mysterious draw of the wind. It moved me further and further as I pursued the steps of the Son of Man. The wind is untamed and unrestrained. Others feel it too. Of this, I am convinced, and I am convinced that others are invited to respond. That is, should they choose to do so. I would desire that the wind moves us all such that the flame of our hearts would be set ablaze. Indeed, there was a triune testimony on this journey. I saw the footprints, I felt the wind, and I gleaned wisdom and insight from the unseen Creator through the visible attributes of creation. The burning flame within me compelled me to go. I responded and I followed, and still I choose to follow.

What if on the continuation of my journey I don't get everything right? What if I say the wrong things or teach that which is false? May it be so, oh Lord, that I may not get everything perfectly right, but I pray that my heart can perfectly be in the right place before you when I act and speak on your behalf. Oh Lord, I simply cannot get this right without you. I will continue this journey.

May our ways be conformed to the ways of our Creator, Shepherd, and Comforter until we are all united under one purpose, one path, one mission. As we follow, and as we bear fruit, inevitably we "go." At times, we will feel all alone, yet we will remain in unity with all of God's people who are on this same pilgrim path together. Separately we will remain united together as we all pursue the same goal of our journey. Truly this journey is not about a destination, but rather, it is about a path and a process resulting in the great and mighty work of formation and transformation. May we be forever grateful for the path and journey we follow, as it will continue to be an example and story of transformation for others. There will be those who will come after us. May they find the strength, courage, and perseverance to faithfully follow the wind and the footprints in the way of Mathetes.